Melody Bober

TUNES IN TRANSIT

Notes from the Publisher

Composers in Focus is a series of original piano collections celebrating the creative artistry of contemporary composers. It is through the work of these composers that the piano teaching repertoire is enlarged and enhanced.

It is my hope that students, teachers, and all others who experience this music will be enriched and inspired.

Frank J Hackinson

Frank J. Hackinson, Publisher

Notes from the Composer

Do you teach students who enjoy playing upbeat, energetic pieces? *Tunes in Transit* is a suite of four compositions created specifically with those students in mind.

Through strong rhythmic vitality and an assortment of technical challenges, these pieces will entertain as well as motivate your students.

Enjoy,

Melody Bober

Melody Bober

Contents

Boogie-woogie Choo-choo

*Can you hear the train chugging along the tracks through
the left-hand ostinato? Play this piece medium-fast in boogie style.*

Melody Bober

FF1225

Steamboat Swing

*Many years ago, the steamboat was a source of both transportation and music; jazz bands
would often provide music for the passengers on board. Perform this piece in a laid-back swing style.*

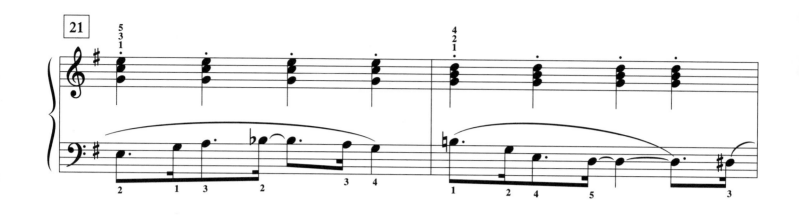

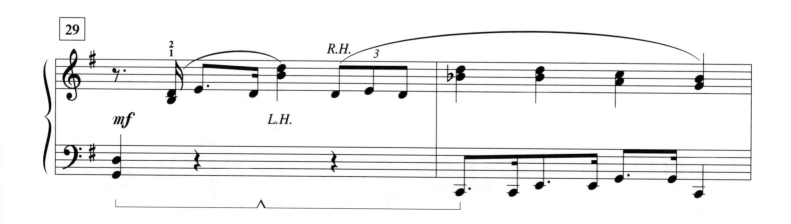

Road Rally Rock

Imagine going to the races and cheering as the cars speed by
toward the finish line. "Rock" this piece with the energy of a racecar!

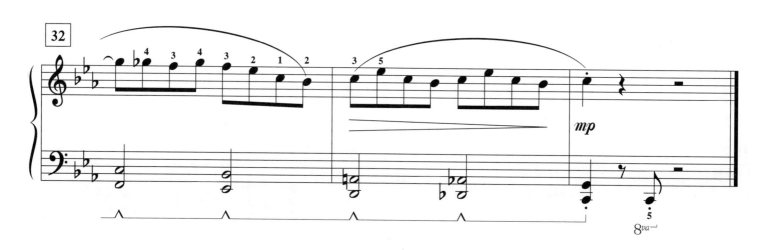

Trolley Toccata

*Let your fingers ride the keys as you imagine riding a trolley
car up, down, and around city streets. Play quickly and smoothly.*

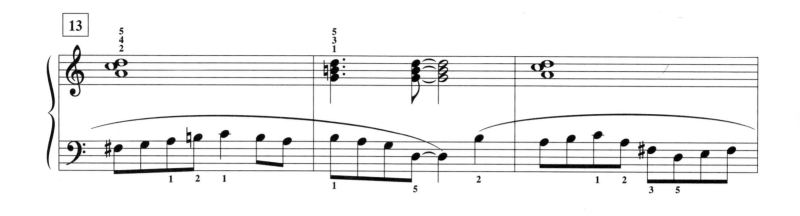

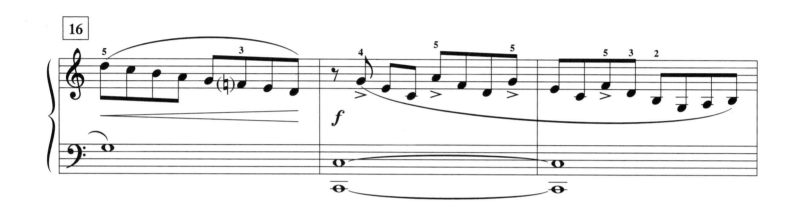

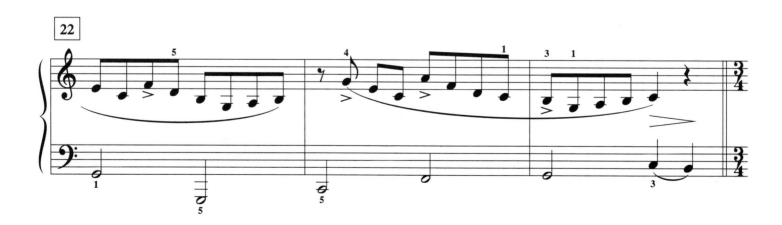

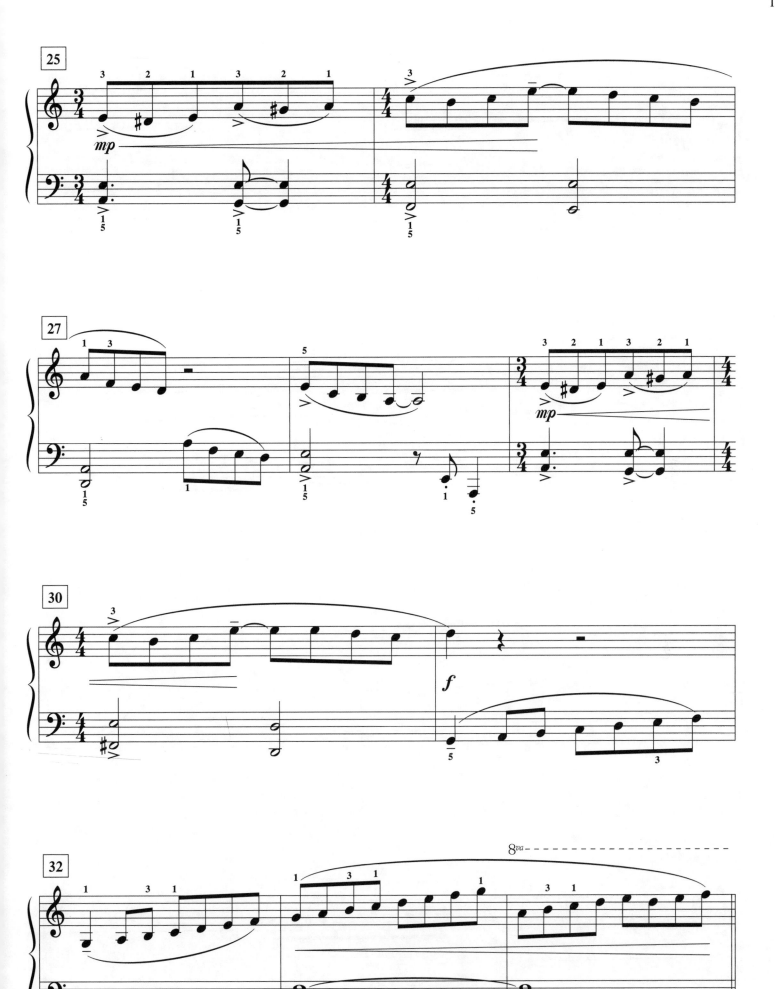

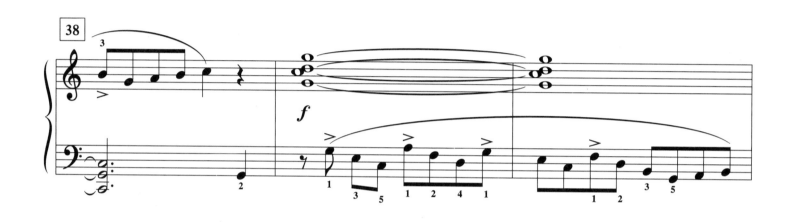

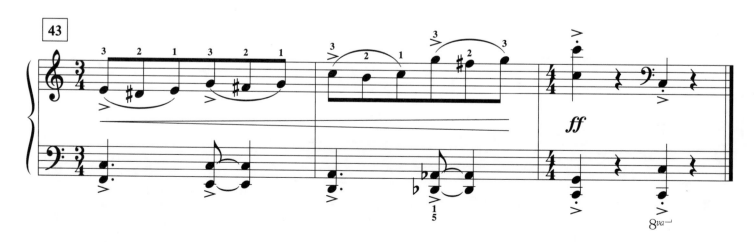